PEGASUS ENCYCLOPEDIA LIBRARY

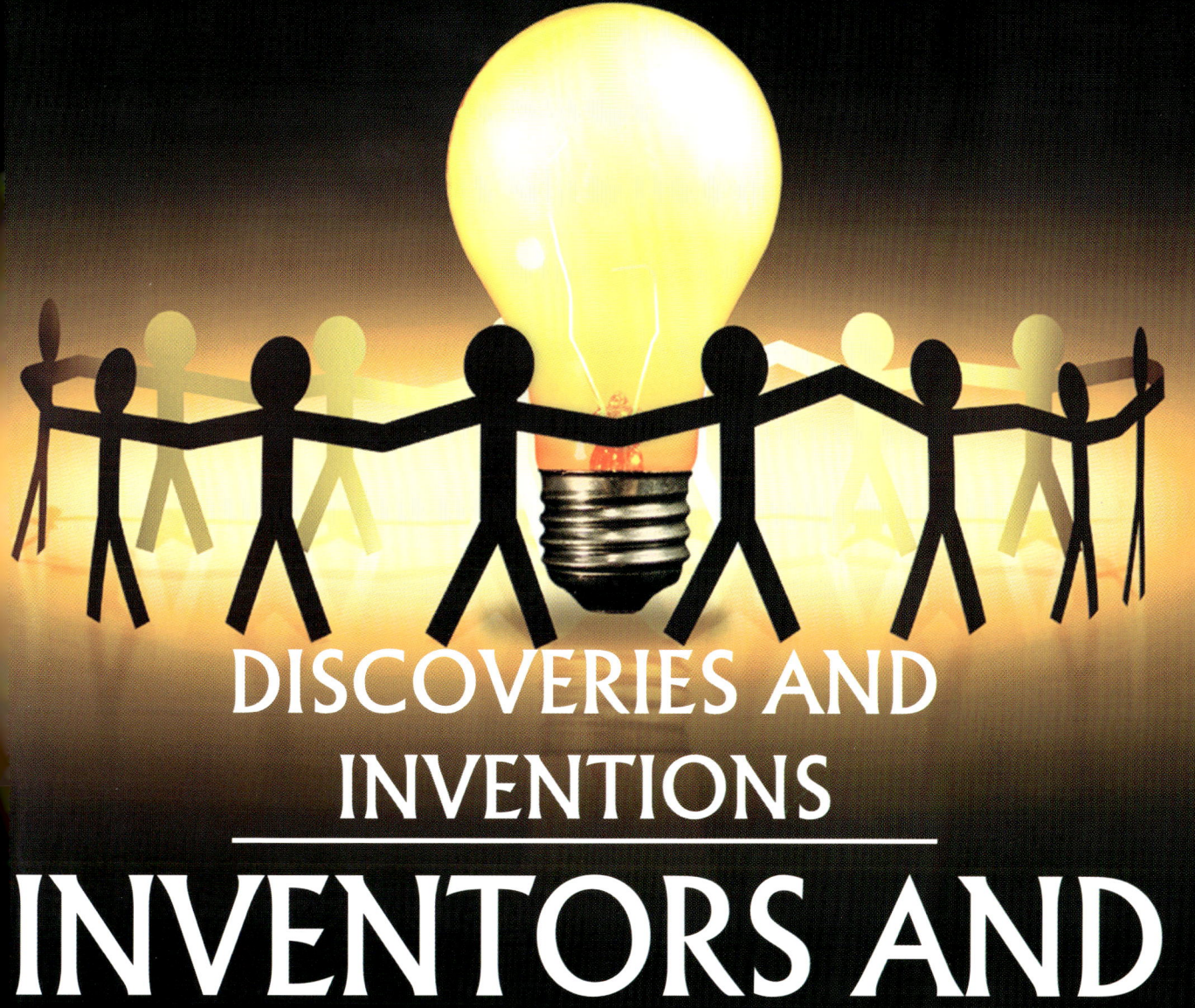

DISCOVERIES AND INVENTIONS

INVENTORS AND INVENTIONS

Edited by: Anil Kumar Tomar, Pallabi B. Tomar
Managing editor: Tapasi De
Designed by: Vijesh Chahal, Anil Kumar, Rohit Kumar
Illustrated by: Suman S. Roy, Tanoy Choudhury
Colouring done by: Vinay Kumar, Sonu, Kiran Kumari & Pradeep Kumar

CONTENTS

Inventions 3

- Compound microscope — 4
- Thermometer and Telescope — 5
- Adding machine — 6
- Barometer — 7
- Steam engine — 8
- Bifocal spectacles — 9
- Smallpox vaccination and Electric battery — 10
- Printing Press — 11
- Stethoscope and Galvanometer — 12
- Electric motor — 13
- Friction match — 14
- Typewriter — 15
- Braille printing and Sewing machine — 16
- Microphones and Television — 17
- Electric Lamp — 18
- Bicycle and Fountain pen — 19
- Telephone — 20
- Automobile engine — 21
- Kodak camera — 22
- Radio and Diesel engine — 23
- Aeroplane — 24
- Air conditioning — 25
- The guitar — 26
- Helicopter — 27
- Parachute — 28
- Blue Jeans and Electric Washing machine — 29
- Compact disc — 30

Test Your Memory 3

Index 32

Inventions

It has always been a great topic of debate whether scientific inventions are a boon or curse for us. No one can deny the fact that science and modern inventions have indeed been a blessing for mankind. We should always be grateful to scientists and inventors like Thomas Edison, James Watt and hundreds of other pioneers who carried out innumerable experiments with zeal and perseverance for the inventions of various gadgets and appliances that have made our life easier and entertaining. If science is a curse it is only because men with a criminal bent of mind misuse it for their own selfish ends.

This book lists some of the greatest inventions of all the times.

INVENTORS AND INVENTIONS

Anthony Van Leeuwenhoek

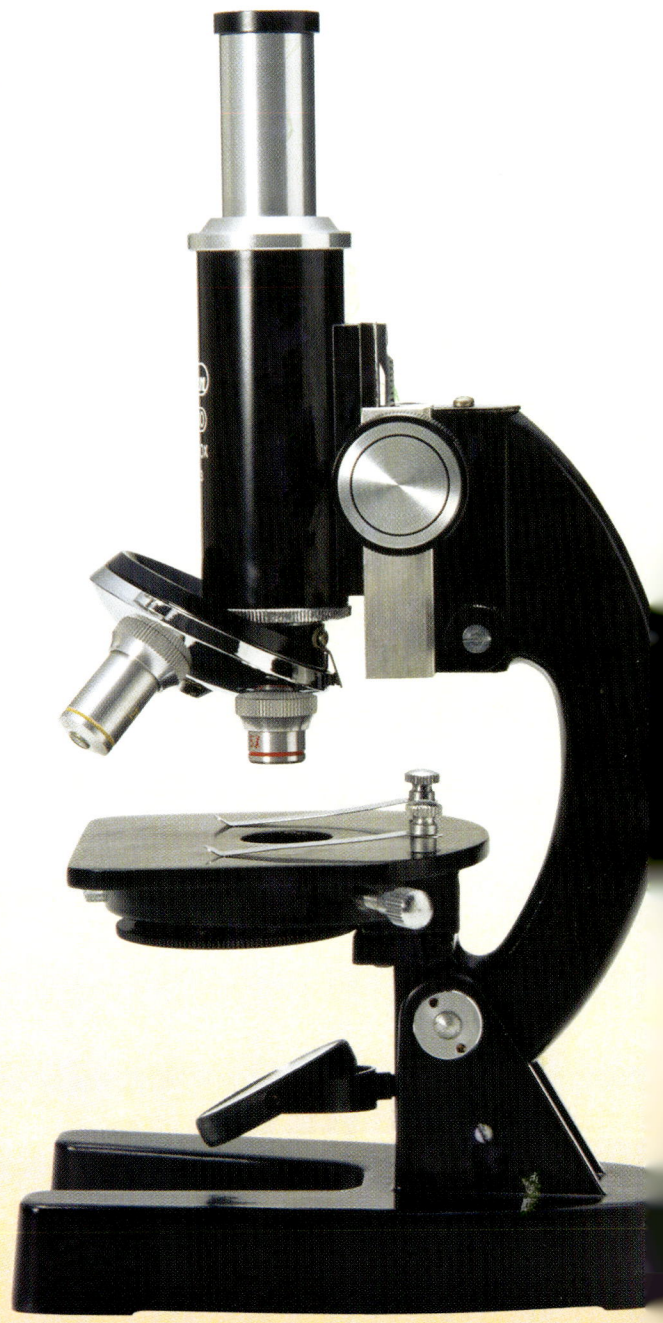

Compound microscope

A compound microscope is an instrument that uses combination of two or more lenses to produce magnified images of small objects. Zaccharias Hanssen invented the first microscope in 1590. He used several lenses in a tube and found that the object at the end of the tube was magnified significantly beyond the capability of a magnifying glass. This was the beginning of microscopy and he proposed that an image magnified by a single lens can be further magnified by a second lens. Anthony Van Leeuwenhoek took microscopy to higher levels and invented many microscopes with highly improved resolving power. He constructed more than 100 microscopes and is known as the father of microscopy. Leeuwenhoek and Robert Hooke are credited for the construction of microscopes for scientific purpose which marks the beginning of microbiology and cell biology.

Inventions

Telescope

Telescope is defined as an optical instrument which is used for observing distant objects. This is made up by combination of mirrors or lenses which gather the visible light and make an object appear bigger and nearer for easy observation. In 1608, the first telescope was invented by a Dutch lens grinder, Hans Lippershey. Two other inventors, Zacharias Janssen and Jacob Metius are also credited for developing telescopes around the same time. Further improvements were made by Galileo Galilei who developed his own refractor telescope for astronomical studies in 1609. The British scientist Sir Isaac Newton constructed the first reflecting telescope using a concave primary mirror and a flat diagonal secondary mirror in the year 1668.

Galileo Galilei

Isaac Newton

Thermometer

Thermometer is an instrument that measures the temperature. The first thermometer was invented by an Italian, Santorio Santorio and it was called **thermoscope**. He was the first inventor to put a numerical scale on the temperature reading instrument. In 1593, Galileo Galilei invented a water thermometer. This thermometer for the first time allowed temperature variations to be measured. The modern mercury thermometer was invented by Gabriel Fahrenheit in 1714.

Astonishing fact

Charles Macintosh invented the waterproof coat, the Mackintosh, in 1823.

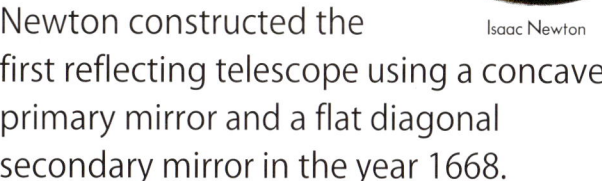

Telescope

INVENTORS AND INVENTIONS

Adding machine

In 1642, a French Mathematician and Physicist Blaise Pascal invented an adding machine. This machine used a train of 8 moveable dials to add or sum up to 8 numbers long and was capable of addition and subtraction only. This device was called Pascaline calculator which was the first digital calculating machine. The addition and subtraction were easy to perform on this calculator but multiplication and division procedures were quite complicated and inaccurate. In 1673, Gottfried Wilhelm Von Leibniz modified the **Pascaline calculator** and attached a multiplication/division device. Leibniz calculator was the first calculator capable of doing addition, subtraction, multiplication and division easily.

Blaise Pascal

Astonishing fact

Music was sent down a telephone line for the first time in 1876, the year the phone was invented.

Inventions

Evangelista Torricelli

Barometer

Barometer is a device which can measure atmospheric pressure or the weight of air in the atmosphere. In 1643, the first mercury barometer was invented by Evangelista Torricelli in Florence, Italy. In the basic device, an air less glass tube was inserted into a dish of mercury. The air pressing down on the mercury in the dish forced some of the mercury up into the glass tube. The rise in mercury levels was observed on the attached scale. In 1844, the first commercially viable aneroid barometer was made by Lucien Vidie in France. It consisted of an evacuated drum whose minute expansions and contractions under pressure changes could be measured by a needle moving over a dial.

INVENTORS AND INVENTIONS

Steam engine

A steam engine converts the potential energy that exists as pressure in steam and converts that to mechanical force. The steam locomotive trains that relied on steam engines for their movement marked the beginning of Industrial Revolution.

Denis Papin invented a digester or pressure cooker in the year 1679. Based on the theory of this invention an English engineer, Thomas Savery, designed the crude model of the first steam engine in 1698. The first commercial steam engine was built in the year 1712 by Thomas Newcomen. Though this invention got instant popularity and the engine was rugged and reliable but it had many faults resulting in wasted heat and fuel.

The first usable steam engine was patented by James Watt, a Scottish inventor in 1769. It had a separate condenser connected to a cylinder by a valve. This condenser kept the engine cool while cylinders were hot. Watt's engine is the basic design for all modern steam engines.

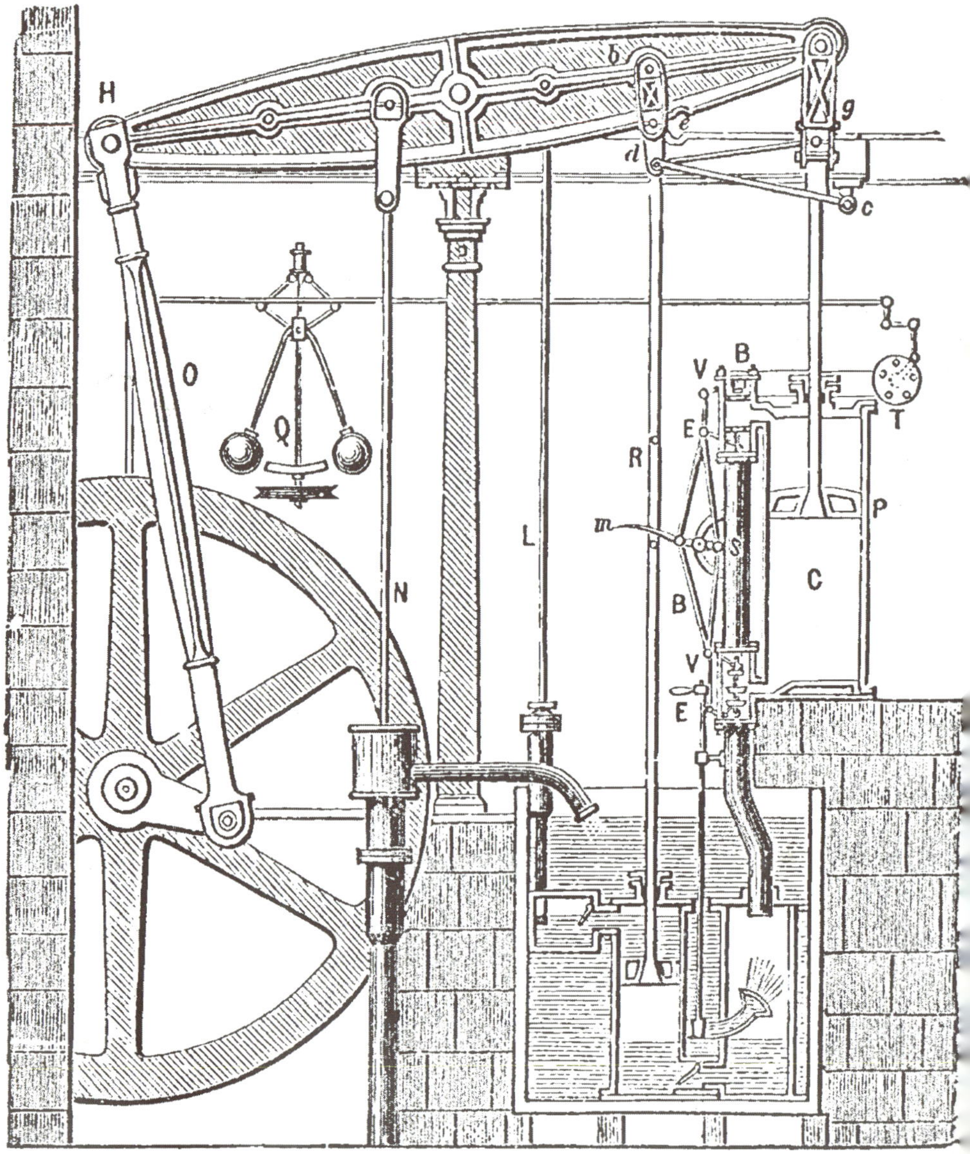

James Watt

Newcomen steam engine

Inventions

Bifocal spectacles

Bifocal spectacles are some of the most widely used glasses among people who have presbyopia and other near-sighted vision problems at the same time. Bifocal lens were invented by an American, Benjamin Franklin in 1780. Franklin was frustrated being both myopic (near-sighted) and hyperopic (far-sighted) because he had to constantly switch his pairs of glasses, depending on what he was trying to focus on. He longed for the ability to see both near and far with a single frame. In order to accomplish this, Benjamin had the lenses of two pairs of spectacles cut into half and put half of each lens in one sole frame. Today, millions of individuals take advantage of Franklin's bifocals which gives them a convenient way in which to correct their vision for both distance and reading.

Benjamin Franklin

Least convex for distant objects

Most convex for reading

Least convex

Most convex

INVENTORS AND INVENTIONS

Smallpox vaccination

Edward Jenner

For many centuries, smallpox devastated mankind. In modern times we do not have to worry about it. Thanks to the remarkable work of Edward Jenner and the later developments from his endeavours. In 1796, he invented the smallpox vaccination. Dr Jenner was aware of the belief that people who contracted cowpox, never contracted smallpox. He realized that inoculating people with cowpox would immunize them against smallpox. He researched this issue and performed a test to confirm his hypothesis. He inoculated an eight-year-old boy, Phipps, with matter taken from a cowpox pustule. The matter was taken from the hand of Sarah Nelmes, who had caught the disease from a cow named Blossom. Phipps developed coxpox and quickly recovered. Several weeks later, the boy was inoculated with smallpox and he did not contract the disease.

Electric battery

Volta battery

In 1800, after extensive experimentation, an Italian physicist Alessandro Volta developed the voltaic pile or electric battery. The original voltaic pile consisted of a pile of zinc and silver discs and between alternate discs a piece of cardboard was soaked in saltwater. A wire connecting the bottom zinc disc to the top silver disc could produce repeated sparks.

Inventions

Printing press

In 1803, Frederick Koenig produced the Suhl press which was basically a powered, wooden hand press with moveable carriage, reciprocating platen, self-opening frisket and self-inking 'cylinders'. These cylinders were wooden rollers wrapped with layers of felt and covered with leather. This machine was considered too complicated and costly by German printers. Later, Koenig was joined by his fellow countryman and good friend, Andreas F. Bauer. Bauer was a mechanic or watchmaker by profession. Together they combined their ideas and constructed the first actual printing machine powered by steam in 1810.

Frederick Koenig

Astonishing fact

The videophone was invented by Bell Laboratories in 1927.

INVENTORS AND INVENTIONS

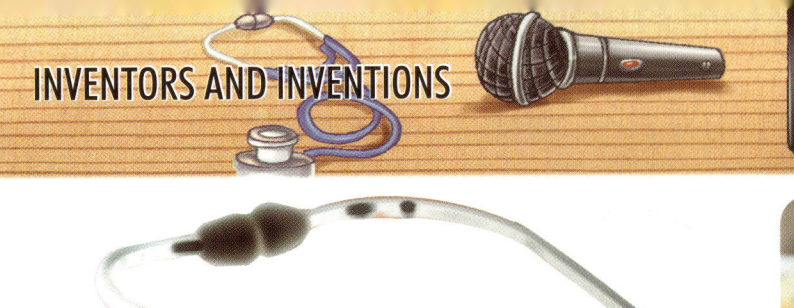

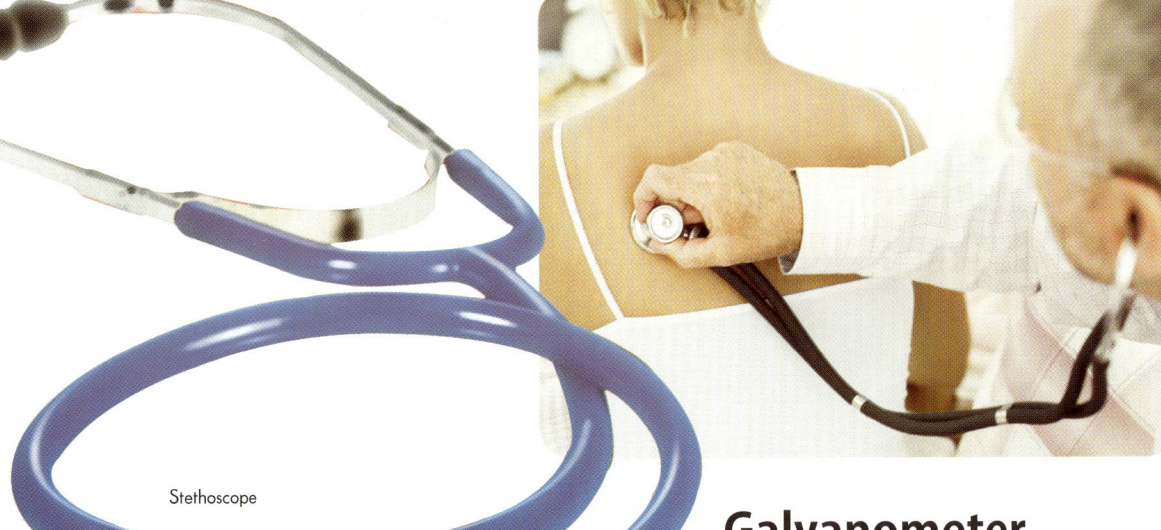

Stethoscope

Galvanometer

Galvanometer is an electronic tool which is used for measuring the strength and direction of electric current. The first galvanometer was built by a German inventor, Johann S. Schweigger in 1820. It was the first sensitive instrument for measuring and detecting small amounts of electricity.

Stethoscope

The stethoscope is a common instrument to all doctors which is used for auscultation, or listening to the internal sounds of an animal body or a human body. Rene Theophile Hyacinthe Laennec, a French physician, invented the stethoscope in 1819. Using this new instrument, he investigated the sounds made by the heart and lungs and determined that his diagnoses were supported by the observations made during autopsies. The word stethoscope comes from the Greek words 'stethos' meaning chest and 'skopein' meaning to explore.

Galvanometer

Inventions

Electric motor

British physicist and chemist, Michael Faraday is best known for his discoveries of electromagnetic induction and of the laws of electrolysis. His biggest breakthrough in electricity was his invention of the electric motor in the year 1821. Electric motors transform electrical energy into mechanical energy. Michael Faraday built two devices to produce what he called electromagnetic rotation; that is a continuous circular motion from the circular magnetic force around a wire. He also proved that if mechanical energy was sent back through an electric motor it is transformed into electricity. The electrical generators are based on this principle. He also discovered electromagnetic induction. His experiments formed the basis of modern electromagnetic technology.

Michael Faraday

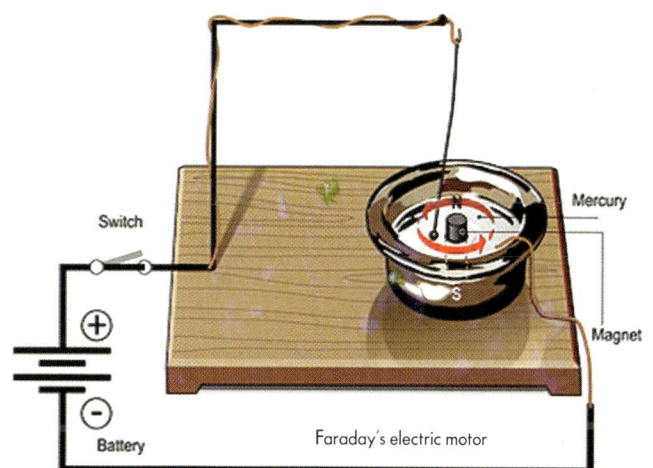

Faraday's electric motor

Astonishing fact

The first vending machine was invented by Hero of Alexandria in the first century. When a coin was dropped into a slot, its weight would pull a cork out of a spigot and the machine would dispense a trickle of holy water.

INVENTORS AND INVENTIONS

Friction match

In 1826, John Walker, a chemist in Stockton, accidently discovered that a stick coated with chemicals burst into flame when scraped across his hearth at home. This gave him the idea to invent the first friction match. Walker's friction match revolutionised the production, application and the portability of the fire. Walker sold his first 'Friction Light' in 1827 from his pharmacy. Initially, his friction matches were made of cardboard but he soon began to use wooden splints cut by hand. Later on, he packaged the matches in a cardboard box equipped with a piece of sandpaper for striking. Samuel Jones of London copied Walker's idea and launched his own 'Lucifers' (an early type of friction match) in 1829 which were an exact copy of Walker's friction lights.

Astonishing fact

The Monopoly game was invented by Charles Darrow in 1933. He sold the rights to George Parker in 1935. Parker invented more than 100 games, including Pit, Rook, Flinch, Risk and Clue.

John Walker

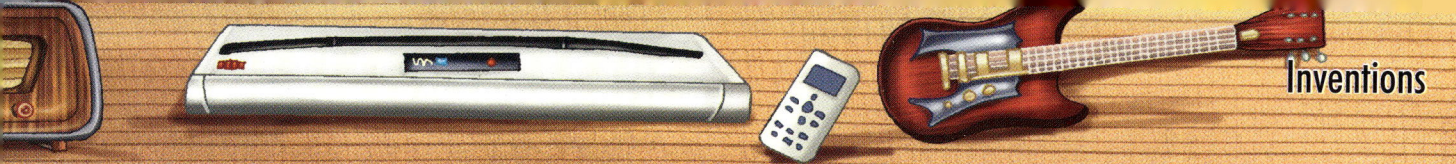

Typewriter

In pre computer days, the typewriter was the most significant everyday business tool for typing the texts. In 1829, William Austin Burt invented the typographer, the predecessor of the typewriter. Christopher Latham Sholes, a U.S. mechanical engineer, invented the first practical modern typewriter in 1868. Sholes invented the commercial typewriter with partners S. W. Soule and G. Glidden that was manufactured by Remington Arms Company in 1873. This typewriter was the first device that allowed an operator to type substantially faster than a person could write by hand. The action of the type bars in the early typewriters was very sluggish and tended to jam frequently. To fix this problem, Sholes obtained a list of the most common letters used in English, and rearranged the keyboard of the typewriter from an alphabetic arrangement to one in which the most common pairs of letters were spread fairly far apart on the keyboard.

Christopher Latham Sholes

INVENTORS AND INVENTIONS

Braille printing

Braille printing is a system of raised dots that is read with the fingers as they are embossed on paper. In 1829 a blindman of France, Louis Braille developed an ingenious system of reading and writing for blinds by means of raised dots. He was accidentally blinded in his childhood. Today, in virtually every language throughout the world, Braille is the standard form of writing and reading used by visually impaired persons.

Sewing machine

Sewing machine is used to stitch fabric, cards and other materials together with the thread. It is believed that the first known attempt for a workable sewing machine was framed in 1790 by Thomas Saint. In 1830, Barthelemy Thimonnier, a French tailor, invented the first functional sewing machine. It used only one thread and a hooked needle for a chain stitch. In 1834, Walter Hunt invented the double-thread sewing machine and it was regarded as America's first successful sewing machine. The machine devised by Walter Hunt was a straight-seam sewing machine which used a reciprocating eye-pointed needle and an oscillating shuttle.

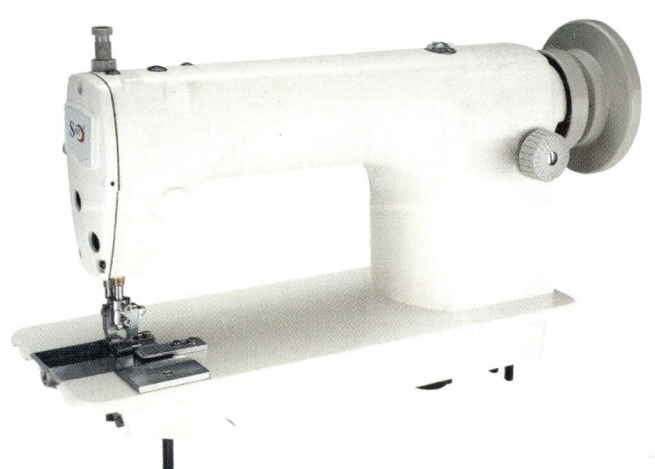

Inventions

Microphones

A microphone is an instrument for intensifying weak sounds. It detects sound signals and transforms sound waves into electrical impulses. Sir Charles Wheatstone in 1827 was the first person to use the word 'microphone'. In 1876, Emile Berliner invented the first microphone which was used as a voice transmitter. David Edward Hughes invented the advanced carbon microphone in 1878. These microphones became common with more technical developments during the 1920s. The broadcasting microphones were developed after the invention of the radio.

Television

Today, the television has become a common source of entertainment in all households. It is a medium of telecommunication for transmitting and receiving moving images accompanied by sound. John Logie Baird, in 1925, invented the television. He was the first man to demonstrate the moving images in London. Philo Farnsworth, an American inventor, is accredited with the invention of the first fully electronic television system. He televised a motion picture on September 1, 1928.

17

INVENTORS AND INVENTIONS

Electric lamp

In 1800, Humphrey Davy connected wires to an electric battery and a piece of carbon. He observed that carbon glowed and produced light. This was the first electric light invented and he called it 'carbon electric arc'. Sir Joseph Wilson Swan devised an idea for practical, long-lasting electric light. He experimented with carbon paper filaments but these filaments burnt up quickly. Thomas Alva Edison experimented with thousands of different filaments to find just the right materials to glow well and be long-lasting. Edison discovered that a carbon filament in an oxygen-free bulb glowed but did not burn up for long time. In 1879, he improved upon all previous designs to produce the first reliable, commercial electric light bulb. The basic design was a sealed, evacuated glass bulb containing a filament connected by wires to an outside source of electric current.

Thomas Alva Edison

Astonishing fact

The first fax process was invented in 1843.

Bicycle

Kirkpatrick Macmillan was born in Coathill, Scotland, in 1812. The idea of inventing a bicycle came to his mind when he saw someone on a velocipede, a two wheeled frame that was pushed along by the rider's feet. He decided to build one for himself and when it was completed, he thought that it would be a huge improvement if he could propel it without putting his feet on the ground. He worked hard on his imagination and made many improvements in the basic velocipede. Finally, in 1838, he completed the world's first ever pedal bicycle. The pedals were attached to rods, which directly connected to the hub of the rear wheel. He was a countryman and had no interest in patenting his invention.

Fountain pen

In 1883, Lewis Edson Waterman, an American insurance salesman, invented the first practical fountain pen. The pen held its own ink supply and used capillary action to control the ink flow. There had been hundreds of patent claims for fountain pens before Waterman filed one in the year 1884, but Waterman's patent was the only reliable work. He had almost spent ten years perfecting his invention. He established the Waterman Fountain Pen Company in the same year. Initially, all his pens were handmade and he sold them through his brother's cigar shop. Waterman also invented a process for condensing and preserving grape juice.

Lewis Edson Waterman

INVENTORS AND INVENTIONS

Alexander Graham Bell

Telephone

Telephone is one of the biggest invention in the field of communication. In pre-telephone era, the one could only speak to someone who stood face to face. In 1836, electric telegraph was invented by William Cooke and Charles Wheatstone for long distance communications. They developed the first electric telegraph for commercial services in England in 1838. The telegraph lines used visual signals to relay messages from one elevated location to the next. In 1876 the Scotsman, Alexander Graham Bell demonstrated a piece of equipment that allowed people to speak to each other over great distances. He called his invention— the telephone.

Inventions

Astonishing fact

During the 1860s, George Leclanche developed the dry-cell battery, the basis for modern batteries.

Automobile engine

In 1885, German mechanical engineer, Karl Benz designed and built the world's first usable automobile to be powered by an internal-combustion engine. He received the first patent for a gas-fueled car in 1886. The car was three wheeled and had an electric ignition, differential gears and water-cooling. He built his first four wheeler car in 1891 and founded the automobile company, Benz & Company. The company became the world's largest manufacturer of automobiles by 1900.

INVENTORS AND INVENTIONS

Kodak camera

In early days of photography, photographers had to coat a plate with wet chemical each time they wanted to take a picture. The process was called the **Collodion process** and was a very discouraging process. In 1880, George Eastman modified the process for making gelatin dry plates which was invented in 1971 by Richard Maddox for photography. The increased speed and sensitivity to light of the dryplates freed the camera from the tripod and cemented the way for the handheld camera, an instrument for instant photography at very low cost.

In 1881, George Eastman founded the Eastman Kodak Company. He invented the roll paper film in 1885 and celluloid film in 1889 which brought photography to everybody. The roll film was also the basis of the invention of the motion picture film, used by early filmmakers. In

the year 1888, Eastman registered the trademark Kodak and received a patent for his handheld camera. The handheld camera used a roll film containing a 100 exposure paper stripping film.

Astonishing fact

In 1894 Thomas Edison and W K L Dickson introduced the first film camera.

Inventions

Radio

Guglielmo Marconi was fascinated by Heinrich Hertz's discovery of radio waves and realized that it can be used for sending and receiving telegraph messages. In 1896, he sent the first radio signals over a telephone. These transmissions were coded signals that were transmitted only about a kilometer far. He referred them as 'wireless telegraphs'. He established the first radio link between Britain and France in 1899. In 1909 Marconi shared the Nobel prize in physics for his wireless telegraph. Marconi introduced short wave transmission in 1922 that marked the transmission of voice over the air or the birth of the modern radio.

The engine developed by Nikolaus Otto used a spark plug to ignite the fuel. In 1892, Rudolf Diesel developed the idea of eliminating the spark plug from an engine. In 1893, he successfully built the first internal combustion engine. His engine relied on a high compression of the fuel to ignite it.

Diesel engine

A **diesel engine** is an internal combustion engine. It uses the heat of compression to initiate ignition to burn the fuel. The fuel is injected into the combustion chamber during the final stage of compression.

Diesel engine

23

INVENTORS AND INVENTIONS

Aeroplane

For many years the scientific researchers through out the world were engaged in designing and inventing an aeroplane. Many unsuccessful attempts were made in the 19th century. In 1903, Wilbur Wright and his younger brother, Orville Wright invented the first aeroplane. Around 1896, the Wright brothers read the newspapers stories about the invention of gliders and the inventors who were trying to fly. This triggered the imagination of both brothers to build an aircraft. They analysed the available information on flight experiments and found that all the aircrafts developed till then, lacked controls. They tried various improvements in the previous designs and started building their aircrafts. They decided to use Kitty Hawk, North Carolina to test the various models they had built. In 1900 and 1901, they launched two gliders but were disappointed with the performance due to lack of lift and control. Towards the end of 1902, they launched their third glider with roll, pitch and yaw controls. They also designed the first ever aeroplane propellers and finally built a new, powered aircraft. After many unsuccessful attempts, the Wright brothers made aeronautical history in the last month of the year 1903 when Orville Wright took the first flight in their aircraft for 12 seconds covering 120 ft! In the next few hours the brothers made 4 flights and the longest flight was of 852 ft. This was the first successful airplane invented by the Wright brothers.

Air conditioning

The development of refrigeration started in the early days with the need to preserve foods. Foods that are kept at room temperature spoil easily due to contamination by microbes such as bacteria. The principles of the absorption type of refrigeration was discovered as early as 1824 and showed that liquified ammonia could chill air when it is allowed to evaporate. In 1842, a physician John Gorrie created ice using compressor technology. The first electrical air conditioning was invented by an American, Willis Haviland Carrier in the year 1902. For his achievements in the field of air conditioning, he is known as the Father of Modern Air Conditioning. In the beginning, the commercially available air conditioning applications were manufactured for the need to cool air for industrial processes. The devices were restricted to industrial purposes and could not find place to be used for personal comfort. The main reason was that refrigerant gases used in initial applications such as ammonia were toxic and flammable. In 1928, Thomas Midgley, Jr., discovered Freon as a safer refrigerant to humans. This marked the beginning of the air conditioning systems for all residential, industrial and commercial applications.

INVENTORS AND INVENTIONS

The guitar

The guitar is a musical instrument having a flat-backed rounded body that narrows in the middle, a long fretted neck, and which is played by strumming or plucking. The guitar is a European invention that first appeared during the medieval period. The invention of modern classical guitar is credited to Antonio Torres circa, a Spanish guitar maker. He made the first modern guitar in the year 1850. He increased the size of the guitar body, altered its proportions and invented the top bracing pattern. These modifications greatly improved the volume, tone and projection of the instrument. In 1931, George Beauchamp and Adolph Rickenbacker introduced the first commercially viable, electric guitar. It was known as the 'Frying Pan'.

Astonishing fact
The first neon sign was made in 1923 for a Packard dealership.

Helicopter

Although, Europeans had invented the helicopter but Igor Ivanovich Sikorsky, an American, was the first man to put a true helicopter into full production. The internal combustion engine made it possible for the pioneers to develop full-sized models of an aircraft with an adequate power source. However, there were many problems that had not been worked out on any one individual helicopter. In 1907, the French pioneer Paul Cornu invented the first helicopter. He lifted a twin-rotored helicopter into the air entirely without assistance from the ground for a few seconds. This invention marked the beginning of history of helicopters. Several models were produced by many designs afterwards but there were no more great advances until another French, Etienne Oehmichen, became the first to fly a helicopter a kilometer in a closed circuit in 1924. It was a historic flight which took 7 minutes and 40 seconds. Igor Sikorsky invented the first successful helicopter in 1939 upon which further designs were based. His helicopter had the control to fly safely forwards and backwards, up and down, and sideways. For his achievement, he is called the 'father' of helicopters. By 1940, his helicopter VS-300 had become the model for all modern single-rotor helicopters. He also designed and built the first military helicopter, XR-4. In 1958, his rotorcraft company made the world's first helicopter that had a boat hull and could land and takeoff from water. It could also float on the water.

INVENTORS AND INVENTIONS

Parachute

A parachute is a device for slowing down the speed of a falling body in the atmosphere by creating a drag. The first parachute was imagined and sketched centuries ago by Leonardo da Vinci. Sebastien Lenormand is credited for the invention of first practical parachute. He demonstrated the principle of a parachute in 1783. Andrew Garnerin in 1797, was the first man to jump with a parachute without a rigid frame. Garnerin designed the first air vent in a parachute intended to reduce oscillations. In 1890, Paul Letteman and Kathchen Paulus invented the method of folding or packing the parachute in a knapsack to be worn on the back before its release. Paulus also invented the advanced parachutes in which one small parachute opens first and pulls open the main parachute. Two parachutters, Grant Morton and Captain Albert Berry, made the first parachuted jump from an airplane in 1911.

Astonishing fact

The hair perm was invented in 1906 by Karl Ludwig Nessler of Germany.

Inventions

Blue jeans

Levi Strauss is credited for the invention of denim or blue jeans. Levi Strauss & Company was founded by him in the year 1853. Initially, he started selling rough canvas pants to the gold mine workers. These pants were very strong but they tended to chafe. After a few complaints, Strauss substituted the canvas with a twilled cotton fabric from France called 'serge de Nimes'. The fabric eventually became known as 'denim' and the pants were nicknamed 'blue jeans'. In 1860, Strauss strengthened the pockets of his trousers with copper rivets. In 1873, he partnered with Jacob Davis, a tailor in Reno, Nevada, and started making men's work pants with metal rivets for strength.

Electric washing machine

Ancient peoples cleaned their clothes by pounding them on rocks or rubbing them with abrasive sands and washing the dirt away in local streams. James King, an American, built the first washing machine using a drum in 1851, resembling a modern machine. But this machine was hand powered. The first electric-powered washing machine was invented by Alva J. Fisher in 1908. It was introduced and marketed by the Hurley Machine Company of Chicago, Illinois.

INVENTORS AND INVENTIONS

Compact disc

A compact disc or CD, is an optical storage medium with digital data recorded on it. The digital data can be in the form of audio, video or computer information. When the CD is played, the information is read or detected by a tightly focused light source called a laser beam. In 1965, the first compact disc was manufactured by James Russell. Russell was granted with more than 20 patents for various elements of compact disc system. Electronic Manufacturers Sony and Philips are credited for developing the compact disc in 1981. The compact disc gained popularity only after these companies started manufacturing CDs for commercial purpose.

Test Your MEMORY

1. Who is known as the father of microscopy?

2. What is the difference between a microscope and a telescope?

3. Write a short note on Pascaline Calculator.

4. When was the barometer invented? What was the basic set up of first barometer?

5. What is a steam engine?

6. Why do we use bifocal lenses?

7. What is a stethoscope?

8. Who was Michael Faraday?

9. Write a short history of typewriters.

10. Give an account of the invention of the bicycle.

11. When was the first aeroplane invented?

12. What is a compact disc?

Index

A
adding machine 6
aeroplane 24
aeroplane propellers 24
aneroid barometer 7
atmospheric pressure 7

B
bacteria 25
bicycle 19
bifocal spectacles 9
braille printing 16

C
carbon electric arc 18
carbon filament 18
cell biology 4
celluloid film 22
collodion process 22
compact disc 30
compound microscope 4

D
denim 29
diesel engine 23
digester 8
digital data 30

E
electric light bulb 18
electric motor 13

electric telegraph 20
electromagnetic induction 13

G
galvanometer 12
gelatin dry plates 22

H
helicopter 27
hyperopic 9

I
industrial revolution 8
internal combustion engine 23, 27

K
keyboard 15

L
laws of electrolysis 13
lenses 4, 5, 9
liquified ammonia 25

M
magnifying glass 4
mercury barometer 7
microbiology 4
microphone 17
microscopy 4

P
pascaline calculator 6
presbyopia 9
printing press 11

R
radio waves 23
refrigeration 25

S
smallpox 10
sound waves 17
steam engine 8
suhl press 11

T
telescope 5
thermometer 5
thermoscope 5

V
vaccination 10
velocipede 19

W
washing machine 29
water thermometer 5
wireless telegraphs 23